Copyright © 2019 Jordan Mayfield

All rights reserved. No part of this book may be reproduced without written permission from Family Psychological Press, except in the case of brief quotation embodied in other articles or critical reviews and with proper citation of the original publication.

Publisher's Cataloging-in-Publication Data

Names: Mayfield, Jordan, author. | Hild, Shelby, illustrator.
Title: I have feelings and that's ok / Jordan Mayfield ; illustrated by Shelby Hild .
Description: Lawrence, KS : Family Psychological Press, 2019.| Includes 13 color illustrations. | Audience: Ages 3-6. | Summary: Vivid illustrations and early reader text help preschool and kindergarten children identify, talk about, accept, and cope with feelings as an everyday part of life. Offers an accessible narrative of common evocative experiences and poses responses from a normalizing and non-judgmental stance.
Identifiers: LCCN 2019951105 | ISBN 9781733462389 (pbk.) | ISBN 9780985283391 (hardback)
Subjects: LCSH: Emotions in children -- Juvenile literature.| Emotions -- Juvenile literature. | BISAC: JUVENILE NONFICTION / Social Topics / Emotions & Feelings. | JUVENILE NONFICTION / Social Science / Psychology.
Classification: LCC BF723 .E6 M33 2019 | DDC J 152.4 M339 --dc22
LC record available at https://lccn.loc.gov/2019951105

Published in the United States of America by

Also available in library hardcover and on Kindle

I Have Feelings...
....And That's O.K.

Jordan Mayfield, LSCSW
Illustrated by Shelby Hild

My name is Grace and these are my friends.

They may not be grown-ups yet, but sometimes they have feelings that are just as **BIG**.

...and that's O.K.

This is Avery. Sometimes she feels sad...

When she drops her cookie on the floor.

When she colors outside the lines.

When she sits in timeout.

...and that's O.K.

Avery has another cookie she can eat.

She can make an even cooler picture than before.

And timeout will be over soon.

This is Liam. Sometimes he feels silly...

When he makes a funny face.

When he tells a knock-knock joke.

When he wears five hats at the same time.

...and that's O.K.

Liam has a mirror to look into.

He has a doll that loves his jokes.

And a head that is sturdy.

This is Riley. Sometimes she feels scared...

When it's thundering outside.

When her blankie is in the washing machine.

When it's dark in her room.

...and that's O.K.

Riley has a voice that sings louder than thunder.

She has a teddy bear she can cuddle with instead.

And she has a special magic wand that keeps her safe in the dark.

This is Piper. Sometimes she feels happy...

> When her mom gives her a great BIG hug.

> When she builds a tower 100 feet tall.

> When she shares her favorite toy with her best friend.

...and that's O.K.

Piper has arms that hug too.

She has feet that can kick the tower over so she can build it again.

And she knows she'll get her toy back.

This is Dane. Sometimes he feels mad...

    When he can't get the puzzle piece to fit.

    When people don't understand what he wants.

    When he has to go to bed.

...and that's O.K.

Dane has lungs that can take deep breaths until he's calm.

He has a voice that can ask for help.

And he can make a fort with his blankets and pillows.

Even though our feelings are BIG sometimes, that's O.K. because we know we can help ourselves feel better.

www.ingramcontent.com/pod-product-compliance
Lightning Source LLC
LaVergne TN
LVHW070122080526
838200LV00086B/233